NATURAL WONDERS

FOR RACHEL AND THEO COBB

PHOTO CREDITS

Star trails: NASA, pages 4-5; analemma: Dennis di Cicco/*Sky & Telescope*, pages 6-7; typhoon: NASA, pages 8-9; air turbulence: NASA, pages 10-11; granite: Dr. Julius Weber, pages 12-13; diamond: Dr. Julius Weber, pages 14-15; raindrop: Stephen Dalton/NHPA, pages 16-17; cell: Dr. Julius Weber, pages 18-19; insect head SEM: U.S. Department of Agriculture, insect eye: Dr. Julius Weber, pages 20-21; two views of a flower: Dr. Julius Weber, pages 22-23; fishing bat: Bruce Dale/National Geographic Society, pages 24-25; roadrunner and rattlesnake: Bruce Dale/National Geographic Society, pages 26-27; falling cat: Stephen Dalton/NHPA, pages 28-29; micrograph of spruce: Dr. Julius Weber, page 30.

Library of Congress Cataloging in Publication Data
Cobb, Vicki. Natural wonders : stories science photos tell / by Vicki Cobb.   p.   cm.   Summary: Describes how to make photographs that reveal information about the apparent movement of the stars, the nature of the earth's crust, the interaction of roadrunners and rattlesnakes, and other scientific phenomena. ISBN 0-688-09317-5. —ISBN 0-688-09318-3 (lib. bdg.)   1. Photography—Scientific applications—Juvenile literature.   [1. Photography—Scientific applications.   2. Science.]   I. Title.
TR692.5.C63   1990   778.3—dc20   90-30914   CIP   AC

NATURAL WONDERS
STORIES SCIENCE PHOTOS TELL

BY VICKI COBB

LOTHROP, LEE & SHEPARD BOOKS   NEW YORK

STAR TRAILS AS THE EARTH TURNS

The earth is spinning like a top on its axis, an imaginary line through the North and South poles. This motion creates night and day. It makes sun and moon and stars appear to rise and set, but they are not actually moving. The earth's motion causes them to *appear* to be moving. This photograph captures the apparent motion of the stars as the earth turns during part of the night.

To make this photo, a camera was pointed at the northern sky and the shutter was left open for about fifty minutes. The stars show up as streaks of light, or star trails, instead of points. Each star trail is a part of a circle that would be complete in twenty-four hours, except that stars become invisible in daylight.

The North Star is the point of light at the center of the star trails. It doesn't show any motion because the earth's axis points directly at the North Star.

You can take this kind of photograph. All you need is a single-lens reflex camera that can be manually controlled, a tripod to hold it steady, color slide film, and a cable release with a lock to hold the camera shutter open. Make the picture on a clear, moonless night, away from city lights. If you aim directly at the North Star, you'll have the center of the star trails at the center of your picture, but it is not necessary for you to do this. You'll get star trails no matter where you point your camera. Leave the shutter open for an hour or more.

This simple-to-make photo gives us real evidence about the rotation of the earth on its axis. Other scientific photos make use of optical instruments such as a microscope, or timing devices, or special kinds of light. Such scientific photos are a fascinating look at natural wonders we may take for granted. This book is a collection of scientific photos and the stories they tell.

A word about the stories. Some of the stories involve ideas that are very complicated. I have tried to tell them as simply as possible so that you understand the main point. This book is just a beginning. If something really fascinates you and you want to learn more, I hope you will find other books on these subjects.

A YEAR OF THE SUN

If you took a picture of the sun at the same time of day on the same piece of film with a camera focused on the same place in the sky every week for a year, you would see the sun form an uneven figure eight. This amazing picture shows the sun at 8:30 A.M. on forty-five different days throughout the year. The figure eight pattern is called the *analemma*.

The earth's axis is not at right angles to its path around the sun; it is tilted at an angle. During the summer the North Pole points toward the sun, and in winter it points away. If the earth were not tilted on its axis, you would see the sun rise in the same spot in the sky every day. All of the suns in this picture would be in the same spot. The tilt of the earth's axis causes sunrise to occur at an earlier hour and to climb higher in the sky in the summer than in the winter. This tilt gives the analemma its length.

It also gives the analemma its loops. This picture was made at 8:30 A.M. clock time. An imaginary line from the top of the analemma to the bottom at 8:30 A.M. clock time would be straight. But during the year the sun sometimes seems to move faster than clock time, which puts it west of this line, and sometimes more slowly, which puts it east of the line. By making a record according to clock time, the analemma has east-west loops instead of being just a line.

When the shutter is left open, you can trace the path of the sun on any single day. This photograph shows three such streaks of light, from sunrise to 8:30 A.M., taken on the summer and winter solstices (the longest and shortest days of the year) and at the end of August.

The longest day of the year is at the top of the analemma, the short-est at the bottom right, and August at the crossover point.

The earth's orbit around the sun is not a perfect circle. It has a slightly oval shape. This shape makes the loops of the analemma unequal instead of a perfect figure eight.

This photograph was made by astronomy photographer Dennis di Cicco. On his first try, the camera angle was too low and the top loop was cut off. All in all, it took Dennis seven years to capture the analemma.

THE ATMOSPHERE FROM SPACE

The earth is surrounded with an "ocean" of air called the *atmosphere*. This photograph, taken from an orbiting space shuttle, shows the atmosphere's surface. The atmosphere follows the curve of the earth. Beyond it, space is black.

In the center of the picture is the swirling mass of clouds of a typhoon. A typhoon is a hurricane in Asia with winds that have a speed of at least seventy-five miles an hour. In the Northern Hemisphere, these winds swirl in a counterclockwise direction. In the Southern Hemisphere, they swirl in a clockwise direction. At the center of the typhoon there is a calm, cloudless area called the eye.

This picture was taken from the space shuttle *Discovery* on August 20, 1985. The astronauts took two pictures from different angles and then laid one over the other. This gives the finished photo a three-dimensional appearance and lets us see the structure of the storm in greater detail.

9

SEEING THE WIND

Air is invisible, so its motion can't be seen. Moving air can be detected when it carries millions of tiny particles that *are* visible. We see clouds because they are made up of tiny drops of water that reflect light. In the last picture, swirling clouds showed the direction of the moving air of a typhoon. In this picture, scientists wanted to detect the way air moved as an airplane wing passed through it.

The airplane was used to dust crops with insecticide, and the insecticide was not landing on the planned target area under the plane. Scientists wanted to see how the air turbulence caused by the plane's wings influenced where the powdery chemicals landed. So they lined up a row of red smoke grenades that created a smoke screen. As the aircraft flew through the smoke screen, the moving smoke revealed a whirlpool over each wing. These whirlpools sent smoke particles to the sides, not under the plane. Assuming that insecticides would take the same path as the smoke, these photographs showed how the pesticides missed the target area and spread where they were not wanted. The sequence of the photos also shows how the turbulence changes over a short period of time.

This experiment resulted in a new wingtip design that sent insecticide particles up in the air so they would fall back on the area to be dusted.

A PIECE OF THE EARTH'S CRUST

The earth was once a ball of molten material. The surface cooled to form the earth's crust, which is made up of two main kinds of rock, basalt and granite. When it was molten, the lighter material, which was granite, floated to the surface and became the principal material of the continents. These photographs take a closer look at this basic material of the earth's crust.

Granite is an ordinary-looking gray rock flecked with tiny crystals of pure minerals including white quartz and black feldspar. You can take a picture of granite under a microscope. Such a picture is called a micrograph. A micrograph of granite is made by using a very thin slice of the rock, thin enough to allow light to pass through it.

The small photo is a micrograph of a slice of granite that was taken using ordinary white light. But something dramatic happens when the same micrograph is made using polarized light. Polarized light is white light that has been organized by passing it through a special screen of fine lines. Under polarized light, the different minerals act like *prisms*, which bend light. Polarized light is bent differently by different minerals and they show up as different colors. You can see that granite is made of many kinds of minerals, arranged like a jigsaw puzzle. Scientists can use this kind of polarized micrograph to identify the minerals in a rock.

Diamond

Diamonds are the hardest substance on earth. One way of measuring hardness is the scratch test. A harder mineral can scratch a mark on a softer mineral. No material on earth can scratch a diamond except another diamond.

A diamond is a *crystal* of carbon, one of earth's elements. A crystal has a regular arrangement of its *atoms* or molecules. The flat surfaces of a crystal and the angles at which they meet reflect the shape of its inner chemical arrangement. In the case of a diamond, each carbon atom is bonded to four other carbon atoms. They take the shape of a four-sided pyramid called a tetrahedron. All the angles and sides of a tetrahedron are equal. The bonds between the carbon atoms are extremely strong and not easily broken. The tetrahedrons fit together like blocks, pointing up and down, sharing the square base. So the crystal is made of millions of tetrahedron units connected by powerful bonds between carbon atoms. A rough diamond crystal occasionally is close to a perfect tetrahedron, as shown in the small photo. It is the strong bonds between carbon atoms and the repeated tetrahedron structure that makes diamonds so hard.

This beautiful, large micrograph was made with polarized light. The boundaries of the tetrahedrons act as prisms, interfering with the light and showing up as black outlines on the surface of the uncut crystal. The repeated triangles are evidence of the internal structure of the diamond crystal.

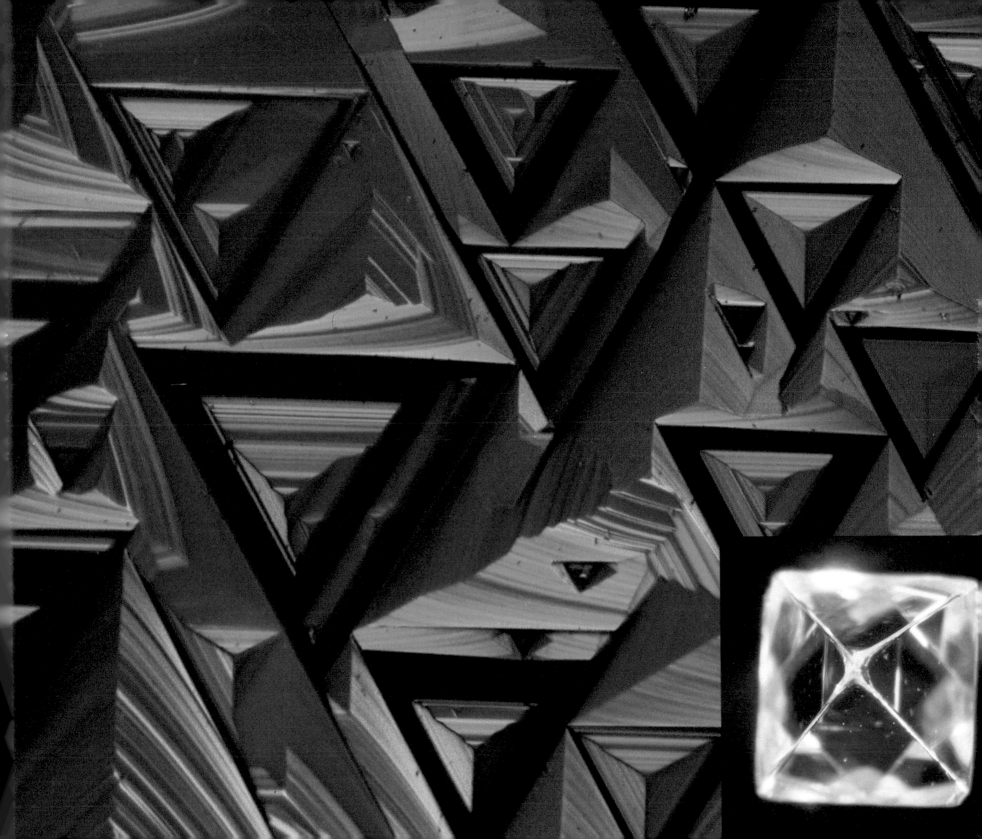

A DROP OF RAIN

This sequence of photographs captures a drop of rain landing on a pond. It was made with a high-speed flashing light called a stroboscope, or "strobe" for short. The images are caught when the strobe flashes, and the sequence has the effect of slowing down time and capturing moments that normally pass too quickly to be seen.

The first photo shows the drop a fraction of a second before it lands. Note that the drop is perfectly spherical, not tear-shaped as it is often imagined to be. In nature, when there are no distorting forces such as wind resistance, a liquid takes the shape of a sphere.

In the second photo, just after impact, .025 second later, the drop causes a coronet of water to rise around the point of impact. In the third photo, .025 second later, the coronet has collapsed and a column of water rises at the point of impact. A bead of water breaks off the tip of the column. In the fourth photo, the column has collapsed and the bead of water is falling back to the surface. Ripples spread in widening circles—predictable wave motion set up by the force of the drop's impact on the pond surface. The whole sequence takes place within .15 second.

The force of a raindrop may not seem like much. But rain, along with ice, waves, and running water, has over millions of years helped break down granite into sand.

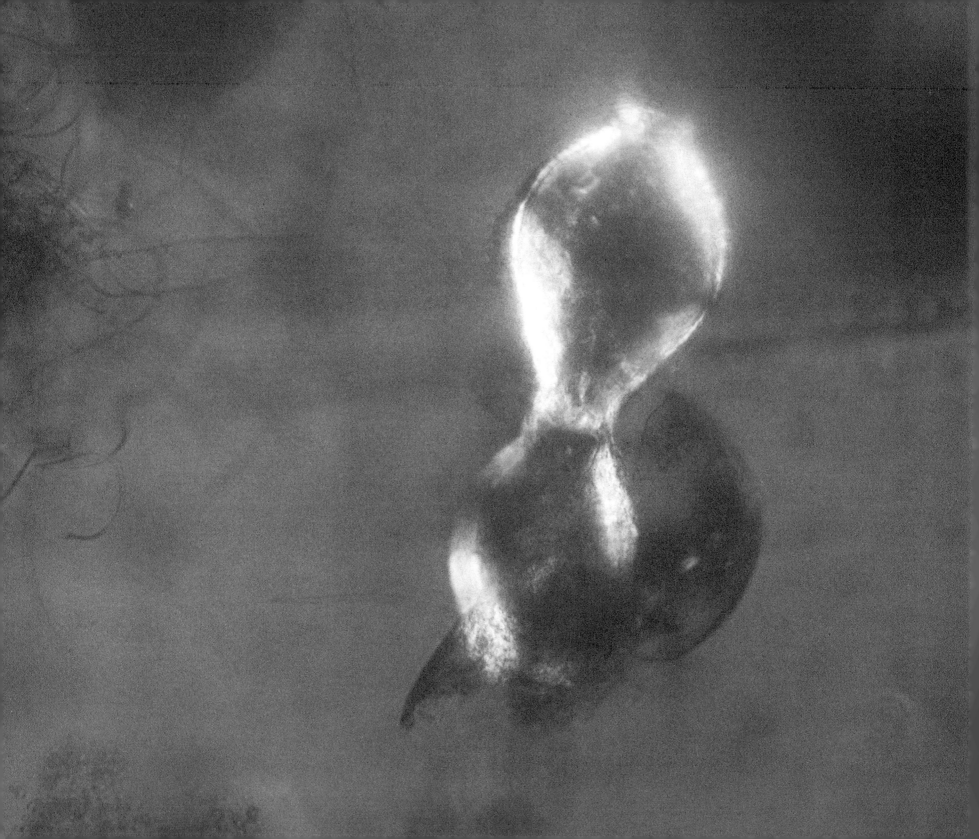

A LIVING CELL

The microscope reveals that a drop of pond water contains living things. The simplest kinds of living things are made up of a single unit of life, the *cell*. All living things are made of cells. More complicated living things such as trees, horses, fish, and people are all multicelled organisms made of many kinds of specialized cells doing different jobs.

This micrograph was taken by putting a drop of pond water under a microscope. It shows one of the simplest kinds of animal, a one-celled organism called a protozoan. Protozoa are able to take in food, move from one place to another, and react to certain changes in their environment. Protozoa are transparent. Like all cells, protozoa have a central structure called a *nucleus*, which is slightly visible in the center of this cell. Polarized light was used to make the boundaries of the cell and its nucleus more visible.

One of the most important things that distinguishes living things from nonliving is the ability to make copies of themselves, or reproduce. This protozoan is in the act of reproducing itself by dividing into two cells. The cell division is almost complete. This kind of reproduction involves only one parent and is called asexual reproduction. Multicelled organisms like you replace most body cells, such as those of the skin, liver, and blood, through asexual reproduction.

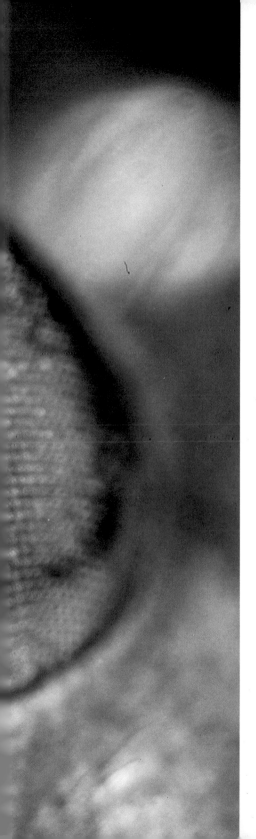

AN INSECT'S EYE

In multicelled organisms, specialized cells are sometimes organized into specialized organs. A protozoan may be somewhat sensitive to light. But an insect's eye is an organ that can see precise images. It needs to see well because it moves so quickly.

The black-and-white photo of a fly's head was taken with a special microscope that uses a beam of electrons moving back and forth quickly over a surface instead of light. The image appears on a television screen. The microscope is called a scanning electron microscope, and the photo is called a scanning electron micrograph, or SEM. All SEMs are black and white unless color is added later. The color photo of a fly's eye was taken through a regular light microscope.

Each of the thousands of sections of an insect's eye is a separate eye in itself. Each eye section sees a separate image, a piece of the whole, which is like a jigsaw puzzle. Somehow the brain of the insect integrates the thousands of images, perhaps into a single image, just as your brain integrates the images from two eyes into a single image. The large size of the fly's eyes compared to its head is an indication of how important vision is to a fly. Scientists believe that the *compound eye* of insects is especially acute for short distances. **21**

AN INSECT'S VIEW OF A FLOWER

Many insects feed on the *nectar* of flowers. Flowers, in turn, need insects. When an insect collects nectar, it is dusted with pollen, the powdery male reproductive cells of a plant. As an insect moves from flower to flower, it spreads the pollen on the female flower parts. Now seeds will form. Many species of plants depend on pollinators, such as insects, for their survival.

What is it about a flower that attracts an insect? Certainly it must be noticeable. Having bright color is one way to be noticed, but, as it turns out, what is bright for us is not necessarily bright for an

insect. Scientists have analyzed the *pigments* in the back of insects' eyes and discovered that they absorb *ultraviolet light,* which we can't see at all. Certain flowers reflect ultraviolet light, and it is these ultraviolet colors that an insect sees. This is one small way in which two different kinds of living things have adapted to each other for mutual benefit.

The photo on the left shows an orchid as we see it. The photo on the right was taken under ultraviolet light and shows the orchid more or less as an insect sees it.

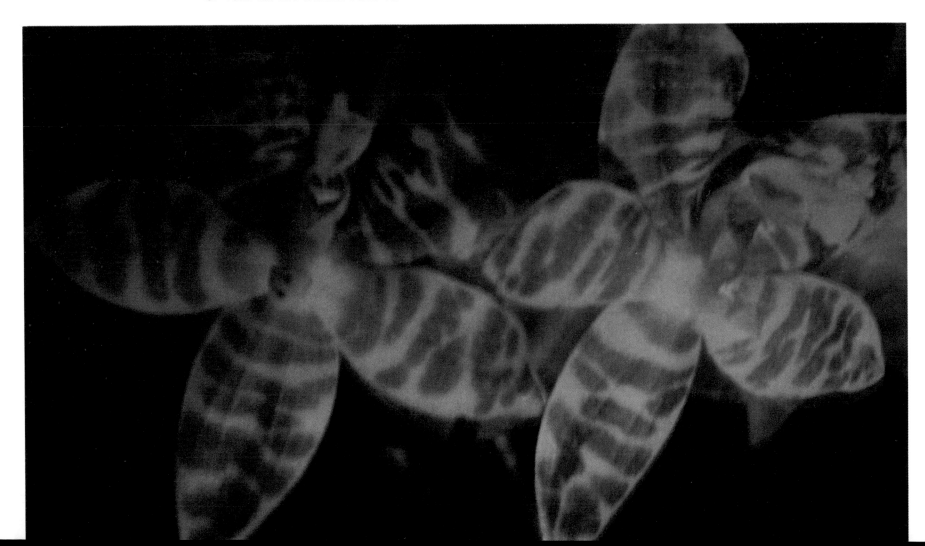

NATURAL ENEMIES

There have been many stories of battles on southwestern American deserts between roadrunners and rattlesnakes. Roadrunners, which measure about sixteen inches from head to tail, can't fly. But they are the fastest-running birds on the North American continent, clocked at twenty miles an hour. Rattlesnakes are famous for their deadly, venomous bites. Both are predators; that is, they kill to eat. But the roadrunner is much more likely to make a meal of a rattlesnake than the other way around. The roadrunner attacks by kicking and biting at the rattlesnake's head. The bird moves so quickly that the rattlesnake wears itself out trying to strike at it.

It's one thing to report such encounters. Getting a photograph is another matter. You can't just walk out on the desert with a camera and hope to get lucky.

This photograph was taken by Bruce Dale of *National Geographic*. Nature photography often requires cleverness and patience. Bruce first made a model roadrunner with a moving tail and mounted it on a remote-control toy tank. Also mounted on the tank was a tape recorder that played female roadrunner calls, and a camera for close-ups. He then placed a rattlesnake underneath the decoy, where it was content to remain, hidden from the searing desert sun.

Bruce waited nearby with another camera with a *telephoto* lens. Before long, the cooing, tail-waving decoy attracted a male roadrunner. At that point, Bruce moved the tank, exposing the rattlesnake. The battle began.

Eventually, the snake coiled its body around its own head, hiding it. The roadrunner no longer had a target to peck at and left.

FISHING BAT

Bats fly at night using a kind of *sonar* to navigate, depending on their ears instead of their eyes to find their way. They send out high-pitched sounds and interpret the echoes, which tell them where there are obstacles and where there is prey. This method of navigation is called echolocation.

The sounds bats make are mostly too high-pitched for humans to hear. All you'd be able to hear are a series of clicks. But the system of echolocation is amazingly accurate. Many bats use it to catch insects in flight.

The bat in this photograph is native to Mexico and South America and is known for its fishing ability. It flies back and forth, close to the surface of a pond, searching for ripples that might be caused by a fish. Its claws are ready to hook the fish, which it will carry away in its mouth. Fishing by echolocation is not easy, and the bat gets lucky only once in a while. Sometimes it eats insects, a less appetizing meal for this bat.

Photographing a fast-moving animal in the dark is not easy, either. This photograph of a bat fishing was made at a zoo. The bat was in darkness, and the image was caught on film during the momentary flash of a strobe light. The photographer took many exposures to increase the chance of revealing the animal at the moment it hooked a fish. Scientists rely on this kind of photography for a precise look at the behavior of this unusual animal.

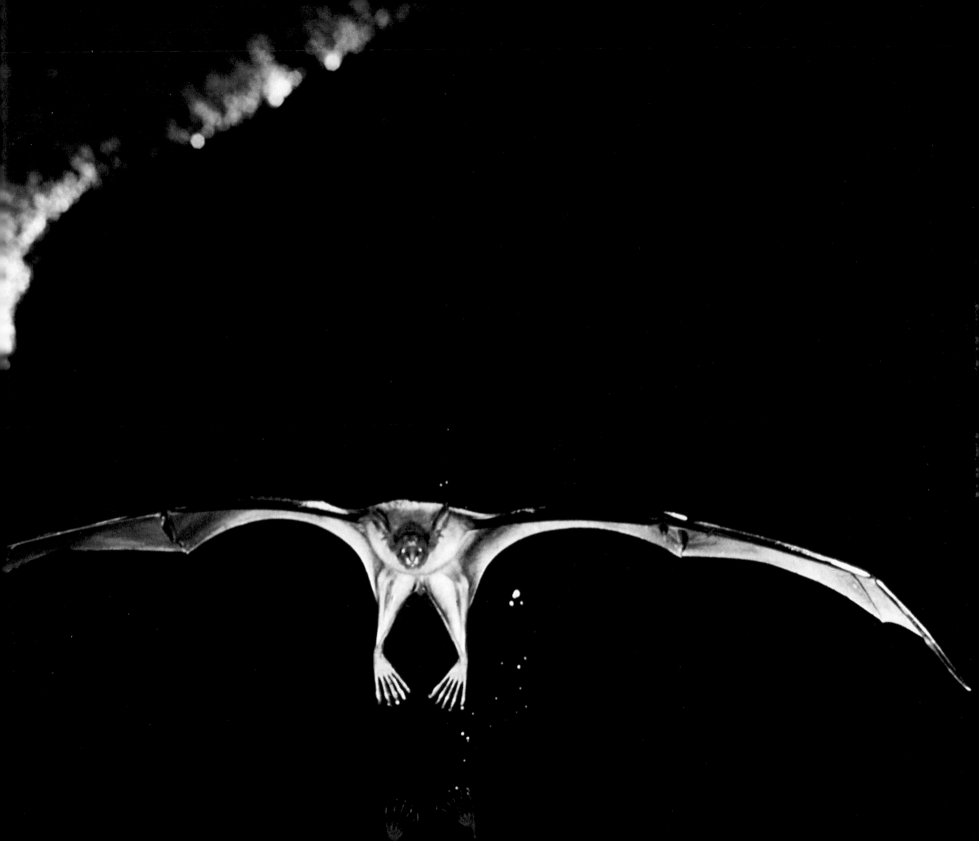

Falling cat

There may be some truth to the saying that a cat has nine lives. These multiple-exposure strobe photos of a falling cat show how it manages to land on its feet. A cat's spine is very flexible, and within the first split seconds of its fall the cat rotates the front part of its body so that the front paws face the ground. The rear end quickly follows.

Many cats have survived falls out of high-rise buildings. During one five-month period, 132 cats were admitted to a New York City animal hospital because of falls of from two to thirty-two stories. Most survived. Interestingly, there were fewer serious injuries and a higher survival rate among the cats that had fallen more than seven stories. Scientists think that this is because a cat doesn't continually pick up speed as it falls. After righting itself, it relaxes and spreads its legs like a flying squirrel. Wind resistance makes its body act like a parachute.

By the time it lands, its weight is evenly distributed on all four legs, which are relaxed to absorb the shock of the landing. A short fall causes more injuries because the cat's legs are still stiffly extended from righting itself and it hasn't had time to adopt a relaxed, shock-absorbing position.

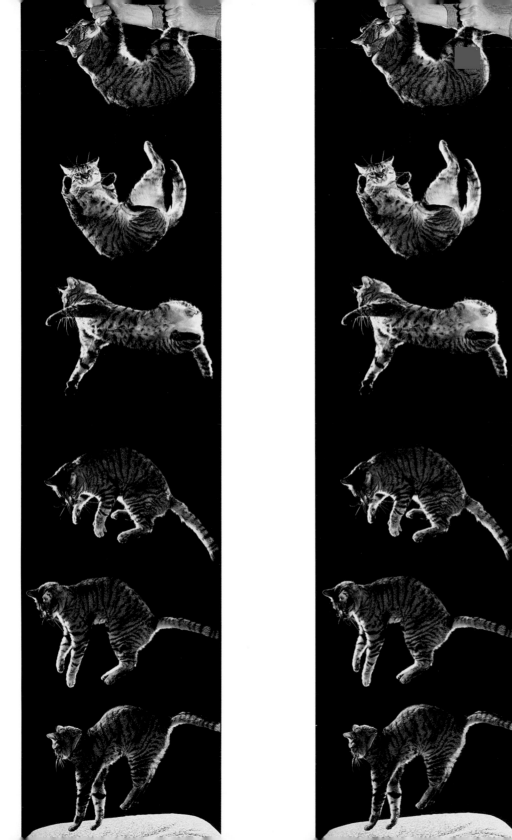

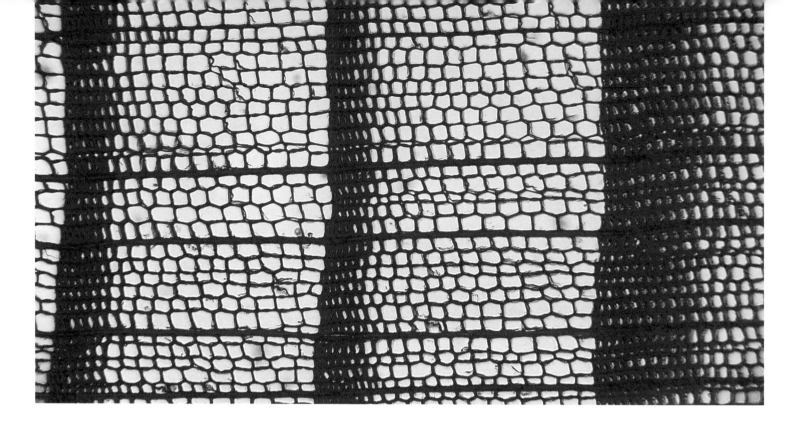

It is the job of science to discover how complex things work and how complex events happen. For example, how does water get from the roots of a tree to its leaves? This micrograph of a slice of a spruce tree trunk shows the thousands of tiny tubes, near the bark, that transport fluids up and down the tree. These tubules also help support the tree.

Micrographs are one way we extend our sense of vision to help us see things we cannot see otherwise. Scientific photographs are an important research tool. We use them to see things that are too small, too fast, or are outside the limits of our perception in other ways. They also let scientists share their discoveries with one another. Sharing and discussing discoveries is another important way in which scientists add to our knowledge of nature's wonders. Strangely, the more we understand the wonders of nature, the more wonderful they become.

GLOSSARY

analemma (an-ah-LEM-ah) *Latin* sundial
on a pedestal
A scale marked with degrees of measurement in the shape of a figure 8 that shows the sun's position in the sky at noon for each day of the year.

atmosphere (AT-mo-sfear) *Greek atmos,* vapor + *Latin sphaera,* ball
The whole mass of air surrounding the earth.

atom (AT-uhm) *Greek* indivisible
The smallest particle of an element that can exist either alone or in combination.

cell (sel) *Latin* small room
The smallest structural unit of a living organism.

compound eye (KAHM-pownd) *Latin* to put [something] with
An eye made up of many separate visual units.

crystal (KRIS-t'l) *Greek* ice
Matter that has a regularly repeating arrangement of its atoms and often of its outer flat surfaces.

nectar (NEK-ter) *Greek* the drink of the gods
A sweet liquid that is secreted (formed and given off) by flowers.

nucleus (NOOK-lee-us) *Latin* kernel, small nut
Of atoms: the highly dense center of an atom.

Of cells: a specialized part of a cell that is essential to its functions.

orbit (OR-bit) *Latin* orbit
The path of one body as it travels around another, as of the earth around the sun or of an electron around an atomic nucleus.

pigment (PIG-ment) *Latin* paint
A substance that gives black or white or color to other materials.

pollen (PAHL-en) *Latin* fine flour
A mass of special tiny spores (plant reproductive matter) in a seed, usually appearing as a fine dust.

prism (PRIZM) *Greek* anything sawn, from the word for "to saw"
A transparent body that has flat sides and is used to break up a beam of light into colors.

sonar (SO-nahr) *sound navigation ranging*
A system that detects the presence and location of underwater objects by the way sound waves bounce off them.

telephoto (tel-eh-FOAT-oh) *Greek tele,* far off + *phot,* light
A camera lens system designed to enlarge the image of a distant object.

ultraviolet (uhl-tra-VYE-oh-let) *Latin ultra,* beyond + *violet,* the color
Light waves situated beyond the visible spectrum (range of light and color) at its violet end.

31

INDEX

Italics indicate photographs.